Three Cheers
for Big Ears

Mary Rose Pearson
Pictures by Julie Parks

Tyndale House Publishers, Inc.
Wheaton, Illinois

To Phillip and James, the youngest of my
twelve grandchildren—all of whom
make me very happy and proud.

Text © 1992 by Mary Rose Pearson
Illustrations © 1992 by Julie Parks

Library of Congress Cataloging-in-Publication Data

Pearson, Mary Rose, date
  Three cheers for big ears / Mary Rose Pearson.
    p. cm. —(Eager reader)
  Summary: Joshua feels bad when the other kids tease him about his big
ears, but then he learns to accept himself the way God made him.
  ISBN 0-8423-1043-6
  [1. Self-acceptance—Fiction. 2. Christian life—Fiction.]
I. Title. II. Series.
PZ7.P32318Th 1992
[E]—dc20   91-39393

Printed in the United States of America

98 97 96 95 94 93 92
 8 7 6 5 4 3 2 1

Contents

One
No Cheers for Big Ears

I don't mind my red hair and freckles. Dad has red hair and freckles, too. I'm glad I look like him.

But Dad doesn't have big ears. I wish I didn't. I hate my big ears.

God, I know you made me. Why did you give me big ears? Did you make a mistake?

My name is Joshua, but the other kids call me "Big Ears." They make fun of me.

Chuck said my ears stick out like a butterfly's wings. He told me to flap them and to try to fly. He made up a chant about me and taught it to the other kids. They all yelled,

> "Big Ears, Big Ears,
> No cheers for Big Ears.
> Yaah, yaah, yaah!"

Then everybody laughed. But I didn't think it was funny.

Once I tried covering up my ears. I tied my red bandanna around my head. That way the kids couldn't see my ears.

I looked in the mirror. *Yuck!* I looked like I had a toothache! I took off the bandanna in a hurry. I didn't want Dad to take me to the dentist.

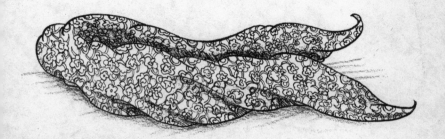

Next I tried on Mom's wig. The curls hid my ears just fine. But I looked like a girl! The kids would call me "sissy." That's worse than "Big Ears."

Why are those kids so mean? Don't they know how much I hurt inside?

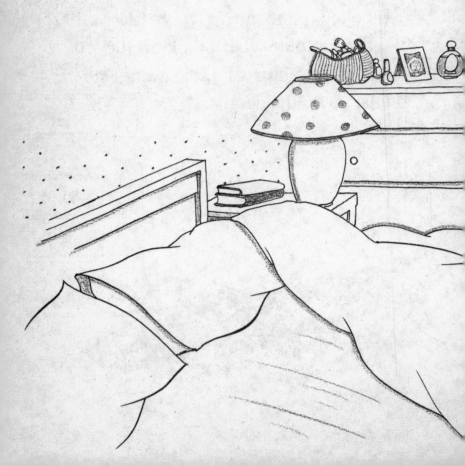

Two

"Be Thankful for Your Ears"

I wondered if a doctor could make my ears smaller. Maybe he could cut off part of them. I asked my mom if we could go to the doctor. She said no and hugged me really tight. She said she liked my ears just the way they are.

"Some people's ears may need to be made smaller," she told me. "But you will probably grow into yours. Be thankful for your ears, Joshua."

What? Be thankful for these ugly, big things? I might as well have green skin and purple hair.

Mom told me some reasons to like my ears.

- I can hear.
- God made my ears, and he always does what's right.
- The Bible says it's not our outside that counts. It's what we are inside that matters. Being good on the inside and acting good on the outside—that's being beautiful.

"Maybe God gave you extra big ears so you'd listen extra well," Mom said. "Be a good listener, Joshua. Then maybe you'll do something special with your ears someday."

I'd like that. I'd like to do something special for you, God.

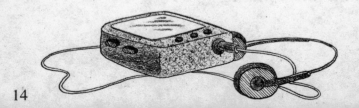

Three
The Listening Game

One evening Mom told me about the Listening Game. When you play it, you sit very still. Then you listen to all the sounds around you.

It didn't sound like a fun game to me. I listen all the time. But Mom said I don't really hear.

In the Listening Game you must think about what you hear. Then you try to guess what made the sound.

"Let's all go outside and play the game together," Dad said. So we sat down on the front steps.

Everyone got very quiet.

"I hear crickets chirping," Mom said first.

Ruff! Ruff!

"That's Chuck's noisy dog," Dad said.

There was a rumbling sound overhead. I looked up and saw blinking red lights.

"I didn't need to look," I said. "I already knew that was an airplane."

I began to enjoy myself. "This Listening Game is fun after all," I said. "I think I'll make some sounds, too."

I whistled a tune. Then I copied the sleepy sounds of the crickets.

"Now I'll make a sound," Dad said. "I'll say, 'It's time for bed, Joshua.'" I grinned, and we all went inside.

There is a man on our street who is deaf. He can't play the Listening Game. He can't hear anything. I guess I can be glad my ears work, even if they are big.

Four
I Can Wiggle
My Ears

One day I made a face, and I thought
my ears moved. I looked in a mirror.
They did! My ears wiggled! I looked so
funny that I just laughed and laughed.

I wiggled my ears for Dad. He laughed, too. He said I wiggled them really well.

Dad said I should wiggle my ears for the other children. What? And have the kids laugh at me even more? Dad said this was different. I'd be laughing with them, and then maybe they'd quit teasing me.

Could that be true? I wish it could. But I'm afraid to try.

The next day I played by myself. I rode my bike in the backyard. I played with my toys. But I wasn't having fun.

I could hear the other kids playing at Chuck's house. So I told Mom I was going over there.

When I walked outside, Chuck saw me. "Hi, Big Ears," he yelled. "Flap your ears and fly on over."

I knew I should go right over there and wiggle my ears. That would show Chuck I didn't care about the teasing. But I didn't. I ran back into my house.

Five

What Was That Sound?

I found some masking tape on Dad's desk. I tore off two pieces and taped my ears flat to my head. When I looked in the mirror, I smiled. My ears didn't stick out at all!

Everyone looked at me when I walked up. *Flip!* Something moved. I felt my ear.

Oh, no! It was sticking out again! *Flip!* There went the other ear, too.

"Look! He can't keep his ears taped down," Chuck said. Everyone laughed. Tears were starting to come, so I ran away fast.

Inside my house I could still hear the kids yelling,

> "Big Ears, Big Ears,
> No cheers for Big Ears.
> Yaah, yaah, yaah!"

I wish we could move far away to another town. But maybe the kids there would tease me even more.

One day I was playing the Listening Game in our backyard. I heard a truck over on Main Street. A horn beeped.

A bird sang up in our oak tree. Then I heard another bird. No, it was more like a cat's meow—like a cat that was hurt or sick. What was that sound?

Six
Big, Beautiful Ears

I listened carefully and heard the sound again. It was a call for help! It was coming from the vacant lot behind our house. I ran back there fast.

There was Chuck, lying on the ground. He looked awful. "I fell out of a tree," he said. He was crying. "I'm hurt bad. Help me, Big . . ." Then he closed his eyes. But what was he trying to call me? Big Ears—that's what!

Hey! This was a chance to get even with Chuck. I could just leave him there. *Step, step!* I started to walk away. Then I turned around and ran home fast to call 9-1-1. After that, Mom and I hurried back to stay with Chuck.

Soon the ambulance came. All the kids heard the siren and ran over.

Chuck opened his eyes and said, "Joshua, I'm sorry I called you a mean name. Thanks for helping me."

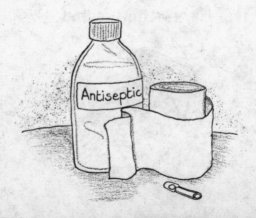

The ambulance took Chuck away.
"Joshua, you're a hero!" Angie said.
Mike whispered something to the
other kids. Then they all shouted,

"Big Ears, Big Ears,
Three cheers for Big Ears!
Rah! Rah! Rah!"

I wiggled my ears then. I wiggled and wiggled them. The kids laughed so hard they nearly fell over. And me? Mom said I grinned from one beautiful, big ear to the other beautiful, big ear.

Thank you, God, for giving me ears that can hear. Thank you for helping me do something special with them. I guess I like my big ears after all.

Suggestions for Parents

1. Be sensitive to the fact that it is very difficult for children to handle ridicule. Children want to be accepted and respected by their peers; but, instead, they may be teased unmercifully because they are in some way different from the others. Your child needs your help in learning how to handle his own special differences or disadvantages.

2. Be aware that many times a child may be taunted for something that, to an adult, may not seem that important. Whatever it is (perhaps having to wear athletic shoes or jeans that don't have a certain brand name), it's a big thing to a child. Sometimes you can help your child conform, but usually you need to help her learn how to cope with criticism.

3. Really listen to your child. Learn what's troubling him. Notice his body language; it may be speaking louder than his words. Sometimes eyes speak volumes, if we'll take time to notice.

4. Try to see things from your child's perspective. Solving the problem may not be as important to her as knowing that you are listening to her and that you care about her feelings. Recall how you felt as a child

when you faced the teasing of other children. Didn't you want someone to understand and sympathize with you?

5. Assure your child that you love him just the way he is. This will go a long way toward helping him face the outside world when it seems uncaring and hostile. You don't always need to put your love into words. A smile, a hug, a few moments of your undivided attention—such things tell him that he is special and worthwhile.

6. Don't intervene in the situation unless it is absolutely necessary. If your child is being physically abused, you may need to step in and stop the action. But, usually, you will do your child a much greater service if you help her learn how to solve her problems on her own. This is important because you won't be around forever to protect and shelter her.

7. Praise your child when you notice that he has made an effort to get along with those who tease him. If he mishandles a situation, discuss with him how he can do better next time.

8. Encourage your child to do something extra special with, or in spite of, his disadvantage (as Joshua learned to do). Tell or read to your child stories about persons who have done this, such as Fanny Crosby, who was blind; Helen Keller, who lost both her sight and her hearing at the age of two; Joni Eareckson

Tada, who became a quadriplegic at the age of eighteen; and Albert Einstein and Thomas Edison, both of whom had dyslexia, a learning disability. (Look in an encyclopedia or in library books for their life stories and those of other overcomers.)

Some Questions to Discuss with Your Child

1. What question did Joshua ask God about his ears? *(Why did God give him big ears? Did God make a mistake?)* Do you think God made a mistake?

2. Why did the children make fun of Joshua? *(His ears were big.)* Have any children ever made fun of you? Why? It hurts when they tease you, doesn't it?

3. Joshua's mom gave some reasons why Joshua should like his ears. What were they? *(He could hear. God always does what's right.)* Can you name some reasons to like yourself, just the way you are?

4. What really makes a person beautiful? *(Being good on the inside and acting good on the outside.)*

5. What is one thing Joshua's mom said might be the reason God gave him extra big ears? *(So that he could listen extra well.)* Do you suppose God has something special he wants you to do for him?

6. What problem did Joshua decide would be even harder to have than having big ears? *(Not being able*

to hear.) Can you name a problem that would be harder to have than yours?

7. Why did Joshua's dad tell him to wiggle his ears for the other children? *(So he would be laughing with them. This would show them he didn't mind the teasing.)* If you laugh along with those who tease you and don't show that you're bothered, do you think this might make them decide that teasing isn't much fun after all?

8. When Chuck was hurt badly, did Joshua try to get even with him for teasing him? *(No. He helped Chuck.)* Can you think of something good you might do for those who don't treat you right?

9. Would you like to thank God for making the one and only you?

A Study Guide to Use with Your Child

Some things God wants you to know about him:

1. God is real and alive. He knows everything about you, even the secrets that you haven't told to anyone. (Psalm 44:21)

2. God made you. He made the one and only you, so you are very special. He can use you just the way you are. (Genesis 1:31)

3. God loves you very much. He cares what happens to you. (Jeremiah 31:3)

4. God has more power than anyone or anything in the whole world. He is greater than your problems. He is always with you and wants to help you. (Genesis 28:15)

5. God gave you the Bible. It is all true. It gives you answers to your problems. Read it every day. (Psalm 119:105)

Some things God wants you to know about you:

1. You are beautiful. (Ecclesiastes 3:11)

2. Being beautiful on the inside is more important than how you look on the outside. When you believe that Jesus, God's Son, died on the cross for your sins and rose again, and when you ask him to forgive your

sins, he will come into your heart. He will make you beautiful inside. (Psalm 51:7)

Some things God wants you to do:

1. Ask Jesus to help you have beautiful actions by obeying him and treating others right. (Proverbs 20:11)

2. Be thankful that you are who you are. (Psalm 139:14)

3. Forgive people who hurt you or make you feel bad. If you forgive a person, you won't try to get even. Instead, you'll pray for him and do good to him. (Matthew 5:44).

4. Remember how Jesus treated those who lied about him and hurt him. He didn't try to get even. Will you try to be like him? (1 Peter 2:21-23)

5. Talk to God anytime you're in trouble or need him. He's always right there, ready to help you. (Psalm 86:7)

Ask your bookstore for other Eager Reader books:

Alfred MacDuff Is Afraid of War
Corey's Dad Drinks Too Much
Harold's Dog Horace Is Scared of the Dark
I Want a Puppy!
Stranger Danger
Natalie Jean and the Flying Machine
Natalie Jean Goes Hog Wild
Natalie Jean and Tag-along Tessa
Natalie Jean and the Haints' Parade